SUCH IS LIFE

Kalliope King

Pelican Press Pensacola
Pensacola, FL

Such Is Life
by Kalliope King

Copyright © 2017 by Kalliope King

ISBN 978-0-9911640-2-8

All rights reserved.

This book may not be reproduced, stored, or transmitted, in whole or in part, without permission in writing from the author, the author's representative, or the publisher.

Linda Wasserman edited and prepared this book for publication by Pelican Press Pensacola, a subsidiary of The Pelican Enterprise, LLC, in Pensacola, FL.

Pelican Press Pensacola
The Pelican Enterprise, LLC
PO Box 15131
Pensacola, FL 32514-0131

www.pelicanpresspensacola.com

Cover photo was provided by Ferebee Photographic, Pensacola, FL.

To the Past, Present, and Future

Table of Contents

The Journey to Elegance 1
Yesterday 5
Can You Remember? MOTHER 7
Mother 13
A Working Man He Was: FATHER 15
Father 19
Dear Husband-to-Be 21
Seasons Change 23
Best Friends Forever 25
Rise 27
Happy Birth-Day 29
Believe 31
Hurt 33
Strive 35
Me 37
A Nurse's Creed 39
A Lazy Day 41
I Will 43
Joy 45
Time 47
The Curse 49
Words 51
The Chef 53
Wisdom 55
Fall 2014 57
Show Me Myself 59
The Curve Ball 61
Keep Your Ear to the Ground 63
Haven 65
The Queen of Nature 67
The Test 69
My Home Is Your Home 71
The Dream 77

The Journey to Elegance

During one of my first appointments with my editor, I shared with her my passion for writing. I told her that—no matter where readers opened my book, at the beginning, in the middle, or at the end—I wanted to capture their eyes, their thoughts, and their souls. I wanted them to be compelled to continue reading. I wanted each line to speak strongly enough the readers could feel without touching, taste without eating, and hear with their souls. If I could not convey written words in this way, I did not want to write them.

She asked me if I knew the definition of the word *elegance*. She then explained that most readers would probably define it as fine living or having excellent taste in fashion. "Those are certainly correct definitions," she said, "but elegance has several other definitions, especially in such fields as science and mathematics. For example, a scientific theory is elegant when it is concise and constructive but is still creatively simple. A mathematical solution is elegant when it is in the simplest form possible to still effectively and neatly provide the correct answer.

"In similar ways elegance can serve you as a writer. If you want to influence your readers, you should choose your words and construct your sentences with the ideal of elegance—i.e., simple effectiveness—in mind. Make every single word count, and make every single line convey the exact meaning you want it to convey."

During that discussion, and throughout our subsequent editing sessions, she has helped me to understand the true meaning of elegance. We have meticulously edited each line and, sometimes, it has taken days to find the correct word. What I learned was that words are powerful. Let me give you an example:

When we began work on the poem "Seasons Change," two of the original lines read as follows: "Overwhelmed by hunger, the thought of a simple meal. / Break the law? he thought what to steal." I added the word "stricken," and my editor substituted the words "he craves" for "the thought of." We followed up with several more changes, and the final version reads as follows: "Stricken by hunger, he craves a simple meal. / Break the law? Bread's so easy to steal."

The change in words brought out details that gave a greater clarity to the poem. When I studied the lines, I looked at her and said, "That's it!" I knew in my heart we had accomplished elegance.

In a similar manner, we worked on every poem until we were satisfied. Since I am very particular about my word selection, and about how I want to portray a subject or person, it sometimes took several tries. I really enjoyed the writing process, but she was always there to find the mistakes I did not find. With precision, she edited in an outstanding fashion. She suggested ideas I hadn't thought of, but she gracefully brought her expertise, clarity, and experience to the book to elevate it to a level I never thought I could see. She has truly helped me along the journey to elegance.

When I was in search of an editor, I became quite frustrated. Not only was the search taking too long, I wanted to be hands-on, working right along with the editor, but that situation was not offered by many professional editors. When I finally found her, though, she lived right down the road. It all seemed so convenient, but then we had to face several other obstacles. My work schedule is never the same from week to week, and she had to deal with several medical issues throughout the process. Somehow, though, we met consistently and invested the time needed to finish *Such Is Life*. I sincerely thank God for blessing me with my editor.

When I was a child, a teacher asked me what I wanted to be when I grew up. I did not hesitate with my answer: *I want to be a writer.* I wrote all the time as a student and on a variety of topics for school assignments. When I wrote on other occasions, I sometimes felt the words "go away"—but they always seemed to come back and "find" me. I would be sitting or sleeping, and I would awake with a thought, a word, a feeling. In fact, that is how all of the poems in this book began, and I no longer feel whole if I don't write at least two verses a day. And, now that I take my writing so seriously, I *always* carry a pen and paper. I have learned, after all, that words live within my soul.

Although I reference God throughout this book, I need to clarify this is not a Christian inspirational. I do believe, though, God gave me the talent to use words, and He has now given me the opportunity to share those words with others. I am full of gratitude for this opportunity.

One last thing: I appreciate all the support that was given to me during this journey, and I hope you, the readers, genuinely enjoy reading these words as much as I have enjoyed writing them. As you begin to read, just know that we are forever connected by the power of these written words.

Until next time,

Fly

Yesterday

Yesterday, unusual for me, I had no words to write.
but I realized, at some point in the night,
the words had become poems to recite.

My poems—now all grown up—had taken flight.
I called to them: *Come back....You didn't say goodbye.*
My eyes drowned in water, but they won't see me cry.
No...go on.... I'll see you soon...when you again fly by.

I WILL let you go. I was the one who helped you fly.
After all, I gave each of you a pair of wings.
Use them to shield others from the chaos life brings.
Then, visit me on the break of spring.

Through every struggle, count your blessings.
No one knew I had words to tell.
I claimed some, however, for just a spell,
and thrust forward by them, I was propelled.

Now's the time to set them free; I feel compelled.
To you, the readers I will never greet:
The words are waiting for you to meet.
I promise they will be short and sweet.

Not a single soul do I wish to neglect.
Not by spoken word but through this line we connect.
Though I know there may be an adverse effect,
I only hope you feel love and respect.

Give

Can You Remember?

MOTHER

At midnight, in her bed, my mother screamed though she knew no one could hear her. She lay awake, her body paralyzed. She knew something was wrong when she tried to get up and her left side felt weak. *I can't feel my legs!*

She caught the phone cord with her finger and dialed my dad. "Help me!" she cried.

"Oh, god, what's wrong? Dad asked.

"I can't move!"

"What can't you move?"

"I can't hear you," Mom replied.

Silence. A dial tone.

Dad called 911, left work and rushed to the hospital. He saw her lying on a stretcher in the hallway, but she was whisked away to surgery as he ran toward her. Heartbroken, crying, he fell to the floor. *Will I ever see her again?*

***

We were not the richest family, but we had our struggles. In my mind, as long as I had Mom and Dad, I could never be poor. Among the things I cherish the most are the memories I have of them as they taught me, loved me, and spent time with me. The years have gone by so fast, but the pictures in our photo album serve as chapters in the story of how I transformed from a child to the adult that I have become today.

Mom is tall, has brown skin, and is as beautiful as she can be. She and Dad have been married for over 40 years and had two children: my brother and myself. I appreciate so much the attention my mother gave me throughout my childhood. I consider myself lucky that my mother was able to raise me, now that I realize some children don't have their mothers around due to illness or unforeseen situations.

I have always admired my mother's willingness to work and her persistence. She seemed to be able to overcome anything that came her way. In addition to all that, she kept a super clean house and fed us really well. (How could I ever forget her good meals? *Mom, would you share with me your recipe for lasagna?*)

I remember myself as a child who liked to be involved in activities at school. Sports didn't appeal to me so much, but I enjoyed spending most of my time participating in clubs and plays. I thought it was cool that, whenever she could, my mother attended my activities. I knew she needed to work; however, she always tried to take time off in spite of her financial obligations.

Mom, do you remember the trip to the battleship USS North Carolina?

My fifth-grade class—made up of excited, talkative children—left early that morning to get to Wilmington to visit the first battleship we had ever seen. We toured the inside and outside decks and watched movies to understand the battles the ship had engaged in. At lunchtime, we sat on the grass to eat our lunch. Most of my classmates had never met my mother and wondered who she was. Let's just say that after several of them came over to say hello, she had "adopted" seven more children that day. We laughed and took silly pictures, many of which included my classmates. On the way back from the trip, we sang songs and played games—at least those of us who didn't fall asleep from exhaustion after our very active day. Several of my classmates asked about her for weeks afterward. They wondered when she would come back again to see them.

Mom, do you remember when I was in the eleventh grade and performed in a Christmas play?

Our assignment for the first half of the year was to memorize our lines for the play. I don't remember my lines now, but I do remember two things: I had a small part because I was too shy to talk very much in front of people, and my mother helped me to practice every chance she got. The days and weeks flew by, and the evening arrived for us to show off our acting skills. We dressed in costumes for our characters and the curtains opened for our debut. However, I did not feel nervous at all. I knew my mother would be proud. It didn't matter if I got stage fright or if I flowed through my lines and got them all right. It turned out our play was so popular we were asked to perform it again in front of the whole school. The local news channel came to take our pictures. We thought we were the students of the month!
Afterwards, we went to the classroom to have a party. One of my classmates wanted to impress my mother with his piano skills. Once again, she had adopted another child.

Even though we seldom had family dinners during the week and never took vacations, I am thankful for the time my parents gave me. Time is something that cannot be purchased or replaced.

Mom,

Due to your stroke, you may not remember many of these activities now. That's okay. I will remember for you and reminisce with you as we talk and look at the family album and laugh together.

Do you remember my glasses? (Never mind. We can save that conversation for another day. Those glasses made me get picked on too much.)

Through your actions, you have been a truly caring mother. You never said "I love you" very much, but I still seem to hear it every time I'm with you—just by your actions.

Let me say this: I knew you loved me from the day you laid your eyes on me. No matter what I may say or do, my love will never equal what you have given me: LIFE.

Yes, I do love you very much.

Care

Mother

She knew me before I knew me, you see.
This is how I came to be.
How could I not love thee?

I was but a little seed she did faithfully feed.
How sweet of her, to care for me.
As days went by, emotions grew high.

A beautiful wife, she carried my life.
At times, it was hard for her to stand,
But she cuddled me with her bare hand.

I wonder if she understood the bond
we formed the very second that I was born?
There is no greater love than from mother to child.

Oh, Mrs. Lady, there in your soul is where wise words lay.
One hundred words just couldn't say
how excited I still feel when you look my way.

She is like the sunlight that's over the clouds.
She quietly says, "You will be all right."
What a blessing! She is here every day in plain sight.

At moments when I feel everyone will run away,
I call out. "Mama!"
And you stand still.

Lead

A Working Man He Was

FATHER

In spite of denying it for a long time, I am my father's child. I am similar to him in so many ways—both physically and in personality. For example, I notice, when I look in the mirror, that my features resemble his more and more as I get older (especially—according to my family—when I put on my eyeglasses). My eyebrows are thick like his, and just recently, I realized that, when I'm thinking, I have begun to furrow my forehead the way he always has. I am proud of our similar characteristics, and I'm so glad that a part of my heritage is to have some of his features.

When I was young I thought he was a mean man, but as time went by, I realized he was just a gentle soul. Some days he carried looks of frustration on his face, a sign he was tired and stressed with his difficult daily routine. He never read a parent's manual, but as he helped to raise my brother and me, he figured out ways to get us through each day as it came. He was also a good and faithful husband, always ready to stand by my mother's side.

At times he would just sit quietly in his chair, and I always wondered what he was thinking about. One day I asked him. "Dad, what's wrong?"

"When you get older," he answered, "you will learn that every day doesn't have peaches and cream. You just do the best that you can." I really didn't know what he meant by that—then—except that I already knew we only had fresh peaches about once a year unless Grandma canned some for us to eat during the winter.

My father was not highly educated, but he had a determined spirit and was a hard-working man. As far back as I can remember, he worked two jobs constantly, one full time and one part time. Although all of us—my mother, my brother, and I—wanted to spend more time with him, we usually had only brief conversations with him in between his hours of sleep and work. He did not let anything stop him from supporting his family.

***

When I was nine years old, something happened that very rarely happened. On an off day from school, my brother and I had friends over to play a game of baseball. Unexpectedly, my dad also had the day off and joined us. He ran the bases and made some home runs. The children all seemed to play harder that day, as if he were a scout and we wanted to join the major league. We had so much fun that day – maybe because we didn't know if he would ever play baseball again with us due to his busy schedule—and he didn't.

I don't exactly remember what year we played that game, but one thing I realized not long afterwards was that we had created a wonderful memory. I appreciate that memory so much and still remember that day in detail.

Dad, thanks for that memory. It was a gift you didn't buy, but giving us your time, in spite of numerous obligations, was more precious than anything else. We learned that day you never forgot about us, no matter what you had to do or how hard you had to work. Isn't it strange how a single baseball game can have such a lasting impact? No matter where I go in this world, I'll carry the treasure of it with me in my heart. I don't know if you realized when you joined us that day, it would be to form a memory for a lifetime, but you did.

***

My father was indeed the head of the household, and my mother was the neck. Most of all, I give credit to him for allowing us to have the same phone number for 25 years. No appliances were ever turned off that I can remember, and we always had a warm and safe home.

When I visit my family now, I notice, of course, that my parents are getting older. My dad is almost completely bald, and he has a lot of gray mixed in with the hair he has left. When I was small, I did not understand that my parents would not live forever. Today, the pain of that knowledge creates an even more beautiful memory of the baseball game and helps me realize I could never resent my father for the time he could not spend with me.

Yes, Father, I must brag about you. You were a jack of all trades but a master of fatherhood. Your strength and your love always sustained us.

Teach

Father

He stood tall…
    in the treacherous rain,
    through the loud thunder,
    under the sharp lightning,
His spine tired, he fought to forget the pain.
He knew he had a household to sustain.

He held my hand…
    to keep me from a fall,
    to keep me away from strife,
    to save me from me.
A wild child I could be in my teenage gall.
Yet, if I needed him, I knew I could call.

He taught me life lessons:
    The truth will set you free…
    Think you can…
    Bless those in need with a good deed…
He asked God each day to give us serenity
as I sprouted from seed into this person called me.

Find

Dear Husband-To-Be,

I thought I saw you the other day. Perhaps you were an illusion.

I think about you all the time, but I don't know where you are. I've searched high and low. Is this a game of hide and seek, or will you, one day, turn to me and speak and cause my heart to feel weak? Will you realize you have touched my soul? I will be happy; I will cry. No, no, it will not be from sadness. I will be glad you have captured my heart so gently.

I wonder when I will be your wife. Can life tell me how long it will be until I know? I must be still and wait for you. See, for you, my love is here to stay. So much to share, I just can't do it all at once. For now, I'll just while away the days until I see your smile.

I write this letter to make myself feel better until we meet, and I can say these words out loud. No relationship I've had has been a "fail," but a lesson learned, another star earned. Each elevates the love that someday will prevail. May you feel the feelings that flow from this pen. Can someone tell me when and where my search will send?

I already love you, my lover and friend, and I already look forward to the new life we'll begin. You will stand strong even when I am wrong. And I will hug you tight when I am right. At night we will kneel to pray, and we will wake to feel the warm sun's rays.

Love Now, Then, and Always,
Your Future Wife

Renew

Seasons Change

The highest pinnacle he had sought to reach.
He took no vacations, did not relax on the beach.
Proudly built, his foundation took a second to rip.
Terminated? Yes, he reads it on the pink slip.

He cries, falls to the ground and screams.
His pride—hurt—dashes the rest of his dreams.
He has never felt such stabbing pains.
He's lost it all. *When it pours, it rains.*

***

Now, outside in the frigid air he stands—
with a restless mind and idle hands.
Stricken by hunger, he craves a simple meal.
Break the law? Bread's so easy to steal.

His feet blistered, his body weak and tired,
He no longer remembers he'd been fired.
He lays his head on the dirty ground.
He drifts off to find peace, to curb the sound.

He dreams his life he wants to end.
Watching a block away is a long-ago friend.
The friend nears and discreetly places a bag by his side.
Startled by the nudge, he opens his eyes wide.

He counts the green bills. He laughs. He cries.
He thanks God and blows a kiss to the skies.
What would mama say? "Try, son. Don't sit still.
It's a chance again to climb that rigorous hill."

Cherish

Best Friends Forever

Sixth grade was when we first talked.
In the halls, side by side, we'd walk.

No one could ever have known then
Vanilla Crème and Chocolate Swirl could be best friends.

Our motto: *Make each day a blast.*
Live every moment as if it's our last.

How I remember your laugh as we played catch.
especially when our socks were so mismatched.

We played all day despite the boiling sun.
We never fought; we had so much fun.

You were as kind as you could be,
always willing to share your snack with me.

If I was having a really bad day,
somehow you knew things would be okay

if we walked to the candy store—
even if we had to return later for more.

Memories: I have so many I will forever hold
of your caring spirit that has made me so bold.

I won't dwell on what I can't see;
I will think instead of your soul set free.

I'll remember you through the sunlight's beam,
or perhaps in a midnight's dream.

So many friends our lives bring;
I have one with angel's wings.

I LOVE YOU FOREVER.
The end of Vanilla Crème and Chocolate Swirl? Never.

Rest, rest, my lovely friend,
for I will be with you again.

Ignite

Rise

She felt a bruise form every time he hit,
his anger so great it covered her in his spit.
A decent lady, she had tried to show love,
but her every effort was returned with a shove.
He ran after her at a brisk pace,
and she never, ever could win the race.

One day, she thought, *I just can't stay.*
It's time for me to go away.
"You are my one and only.
Please, don't go. I'll be so lonely,"
he begged her with a diamond in his hand,
the same that later slapped her 'til she could not stand.

That night she fought her last fight.
A dear friend bought a ticket, put her on a flight.
She had known in her heart it was all wrong
and had delayed her decision for far too long.
She thought she was too weak to ever leave
but, if she stayed, a loved one would grieve.

Years later, she lives with no fear.
and makes sure to keep her loved ones near.
She lives in a house that sits up on a hill.
She enjoys her life and pays every bill.
She feels confident and free.
Everyone listens when she speaks as Ph.D.

With a past she does not want to relive,
she has still learned over time to forgive.
During the days of hit and spit,
he ignited a fire that now won't quit.
When knocked to the ground, she became wise
and accepted the belief she would someday RISE.

Celebrate

Happy Birth-day

Fate is sacred, protected, and sealed.
In the bubble, in darkness, you were concealed.
With the feelings of life already innate,
You broke the waters and flooded the gate.
As light pierced your eyes with its strong glare,
You cried out in protest your arrival to declare.

After you took that first precious breath of fresh air,
the chaos in your ears became an unwanted blare
as you lay startled, shaken, and bare.
Though wrinkled and loose, your skin was soft and fair,
and straight up on your head stood bunches of hair.
Oh, your birth was beautiful, a joyous affair.

Already it is time to start on life's path.
You will soon be walking...then counting math.
With legs to leap in happy play,
I will someday see your childhood shed away.
So much I will share with you; so much I will say.
Yawn! Stretch! Celebrate! Happy Birth-day!

Entertain

Believe

I saw my new neighbor as I walked down the street.
She smiled and said, "Come on in. You, it's nice to meet.
I've never entertained a stranger."
Though nervous, I knew I was in no danger.

God, I now believe she was an angel sent to me.
You sit above and our every need you see.
We should never question your reasons; thus,
each day your angels walk along with us.

Her wings carried me—when I thought the world would end.
Her talks helped my broken heart to mend.
Sometimes, when we walked in the pure white sand,
on my shoulder she would rest her gentle hand.

One day when I was troubled, she quietly sat by my side
and whispered, "God knows your destiny. He will provide."
Although I didn't know what the future would be,
at that moment, I realized that she believed in it for me.

She showed me the purpose I could not find.
She was like no other, so courageously kind.
Now, I understand why God chose her to send.
She was there every time I needed a friend.

She appeared in a world so dark and gray,
but she said, "No matter what, I'll stay."
I am glad on that day I took a walk that way.
For her—each day—a blessing I pray.

Cry

Hurt

The hurt was more than skin deep.
I will tell you, I did weep.
He said to go away, he didn't care.
Such a pain I could not bare.
Was it me?

I gave to him an "I'm sorry" card.
He tore it up, his heart so hard.
When I tried to reconcile by phone,
instead of his voice, I heard the dial tone.
Was it me?

He plotted like a thief,
knowing true love was always my belief.
My fragile heart, he did steal,
and now I am left alone to heal.
Was it me?

It came to me as I sat thinking one hour:
I deserved to be treated like a beautiful flower.
I, as well as any I love, sprouted as seeds.
Water, soil, air, and sunlight to fulfill our needs.

When it's too hot, sit us in the shade.
Talk to us sweet, and our color won't fade.
Our roots will intertwine and through the bonds we've made,
The dew of our love will flow—an endless cascade.

Uplift

Strive

Life is hard enough just to survive.
Those who connive will only deprive.
Persistence is needed to continue to thrive,
so, to inspire others, I must strive.

I have not reached my best.
My mind is racing. I can't be still.
I can't stop. I will not rest.
My heart is boiling with internal will.

When we uplift, we can create a loud sound.
We can shake the earth and move the ground.
We can make a circle and spin around
and speak words of love as we touch down.

If we focus on what we're supposed to see,
we learn no situation has to be bad.
The world is what we make it to be.
We cannot afford a moment to be sad.

Exercise

Me

Watch yourself as you go from place to place.
Try courtesy to others; life is no footrace.
When pressure comes, try not to fold.
Try, instead, to eliminate rude traits you hold.

Relax to relieve the stress.
Meditate with the spirit we all possess.
Rest—instead of brood through the night—
so the body will refresh, the spirit beam bright.

Be extra careful about what you eat.
Skip to keep your heart on its beat.
And don't forget your next doctor's visit.
Write it on the calendar so you won't miss it.

Remember, we are a team.
Together we can fulfill many a dream.
I am your body, with the heart and the brain,
the body you shelter from the cold and the rain.

I am you, and you are me.
I cannot function if there is no we.
Since I don't want to miss one bit,
take time now for yourself—just sit.

If you take care, this body won't give you slack.
When you look in the mirror, I will smile right back..

Heal

A Nurse's Creed

We are a rare breed. To the weak—
when others will not let them speak—
we offer a chance to gain a choice
through the harmony of our voice.

As we smile our greetings along the way,
we go the extra mile every day.
We remember our oath: Do no harm.
Safety is priority one for us. Set the alarm.

Close the exit doors...
All clear on the floors...
The steps we walk through in fire drills
means practice perfecting our skills.

Our healing hands give aid for many reasons.
Nurses at the bedside, during all seasons.
Cardiac arrest. Paralyzing stroke.
Liquid diet. Please don't choke.

Some will survive; others may die.
Lord, grant us strength, we won't ask why.
Time to remember, time to cry.
See you later, never goodbye.

In time of advice or dire need,
care is given without prejudice or greed.
Rapid response to the crisis or call.
In our hearts, we have love for all.

To whom much is given, much is required.

Rest

A Lazy Day

Today will be my lazy day—
with not a bit of work and lots of play.
Usually I start with a punch at the time clock,
but I'll ignore the door if I hear a knock.
With no approaching deadlines to meet,
I won't allow shoes on my callused feet.

Vacuum or mop? My legs can't stand up to clean.
The throb in my back causes me to lean.
Slowly, I walk to the kitchen to eat.
Soon I will recline in my lazy seat.
I'm gonna hide and not be seen.
Time to turn on the dusty flat screen.

Every so often I must go to my nest.
I need at least one day of rest.
Work pushes me hard, as if I'm a machine.
Soon, it will be time to get back to a routine.
I will miss this day when it comes to an end.
One more minute: These limbs are not ready to bend.

Conquer

I Will

I am missing a pair of legs.

People stop to stare.
I wonder if they care.

"Talk to me, you'll learn something new.
I am part of a distinct few.

"Like others, I dream.
Let me show you what I mean.

"I try harder than most to learn
and feel confident that what I want I can earn."

When I can change opinions with a new fact,
I give people a positive way to react.

Today, I have no reason to frown.
I am dressed in my cap and gown.

People stand up to see.
Unique, I am and will continue to be.

I watch—trembling—and wait for the sound.
The audience smiles, and hands clap all around.

I will conquer. I will not beg.

Fight

Joy

Someone tries to crawl under my skin.
I feel anger seep through a hole that sin bores.
I must fight to keep the Joy within.
So, I let Joy breathe through my pores.
Sin still tries to provoke me, but I won't let it in.
Joy protects me, heals my cuts and my sores.

Found in my heart, not in any store,
Joy permeates life—I couldn't ask for more.
Even at sad moments, with tears hard to ignore,
Joy gives me warmth like nothing before.
It may be all we have in time of war—
when we need to let the soul shine from the core.

Whenever I lose my sight,
when the world becomes too dark,
I turn on my eternal light.
Joy becomes my guiding arc.
Whether it's daytime or the middle of the night,
Joy fills me every time I embark.

Rush

Time

Midnight climbs to sunlight.

Mom yells that the bus is on its way.
The minutes run by though we beg them to stay.
Someone forgets their bus fare.
A stranger lends a coin to care.

Rush hour is on.

Dad, in his car, waits to turn in the gate.
The sound of a clock chime tells him he's late.
Though the workday is yet to begin.
he's still not there and can't wait for its end.

Time appears to slow down.

People browse the shops and order a cappuccino.
Around them all the seconds, minutes, and hours flow.
The sun casts its shadows as the rain clouds overcast the sky.
The vapor of life is veiled as the wind passes by.

Time never pauses.

In its constant flow
someone asks, *What's today date?*
Never mind….It's tomorrow.
The sun is up. Time to start a clean slate.

Reverse

The Curse

I once held you, so innocent and carefree,
the dangers of the world your eyes couldn't see.
As parent, I was your first trustee.
But apples don't fall too far from the tree.

You grew up to live by what I've taught.
Maybe your ears listened to our talks.
Remember, a time as dad and son we fought.
A man carries himself by the life he walks.

I sat one day and spoke this thought:
A generational curse I unknowingly brought.
I don't want my son to be "lined in chalk."
I don't know how, but change must be sought.

I cry out to you, Son!

Please listen to me—in and out of jail
I fell asleep—holding your mail.
Though freedom I couldn't keep,
I now have to share wisdom I hold deep.

Do as I say, not as I did when I was a kid,
Past mishaps, so vivid
A can closed by a metal lid.
One place, I strongly forbid.

To you a different way I pledge:
I will help you stand solid and stay away from the edge.
Seek knowledge first, in its depths immerse.
Keep for it a thirst, and move beyond the curse.

Enhance

Words

Am I crazy? How do I explain?
The words flow through my frame,
the last stop before ink, my brain.
Overwhelmed by their presence, I forget my name.
But none of them will ever die in vain
because, into my mind, another verse just came.

I love words, I must confess.
Excited by some I don't want to forget—
spoken or written, they give freedom to express—
I write them down so there's no way I can fret.
Some people care, others a little less.
Very few in the world, like me, I have met.

Having felt their power, it's hard to regress.
Words keep me in motion.
I feel relaxed: no pain, no stress.
Words help enhance my five senses, my emotion.
My worries, my troubles they help suppress.
Words are my secret potion.

Eat

The Chef

My stomach growls. (That's the snack I ate.)
My palate pleads for good food on a plate.

My eyes gazes at a possible meal,
the sirloin steak so fresh in a seal.

Add a heaping bowl of hot brown rice.
I bought the bag for pennies on the price.

I'll toss a salad—leaves, fresh and green,
in the garden my eyes have seen.

Truth be told, I don't like to cook.
Secretly, I learned from a recipe book

Yet, the nosy neighbors I did invite,
requested their presence for dinner tonight.

I sit them around the table to eat.
Nervous, I feel my heart skip a beat.

Thinking of appetites they want to sate
their mouths begin to salivate.

Although we say a blessing before the food,
no one appears in a chatty mood.

Each plate befriends its fork, knife, and spoon.
Before long, someone says they must go soon.

I look around; barely a crumb is left.
Indeed, I see the table, of food, is bereft.

One man rubs his belly right next to his plate.
So… when can we plan our next dinner date?

Retire

Wisdom

Her age, mixed in with memories, crept
across her face.
The custodian pushed his broom and swept
up yesteryear, every trace.

She wept.
I could only listen.

I've packed my office in the one box—
Is this the last time I'll be wearing Crocs?
What will become of me?

Retire? I'd rather work instead.
I'm afraid of what lies ahead.
The next life, I don't want to see.

I'll not have to do what a boss would require.
So, should I do what I aspire?
No, old age has given me a bad knee.

May I give you a hug, my friend? Please don't weep.
You'll have no early alarms, just the beauty of sleep.
You now have wisdom of life to share…
Don't cry… Do you realize how much I care?

Life is just beginning, despite the many years gone.
Though no husband or child, you will never be alone.
Trinkets to unwrap, puzzles to unravel,
Search the earth for *all* when you travel.

Seize the moments waiting in reserve.
So little stress to frazzle a nerve.
Life, now bitter, will again turn sweet.
Remember, you have people to meet.

You've already begun to accomplish this feat—
just by talking with me from this seat.

You and your wisdom are set free…

Write

Fall 2014

The writing pen called out in a voice so small,
Kalliope, you will begin to write this fall.
Right about when people are shopping the mall.

Students will be in classes.
But, your purpose is to reach the masses
and make everyone want their reading glasses.

I'll be the first to read and admire.
This is your passion, your born desire:
to write the words that will inspire.

You will touch people from east to west.
I will help you show others the words that you quest.
When we write those words, we will write at our best.

Words have the power to create and to send
the insight needed to make a new friend.
They also help the fragile heart start to mend.

Kalliope, I am your favorite pen.
Our journey is very far from its end.
Let's write. Let's work. Let us begin.

Guide

Show Me Myself

One word can inspire
if I find the desire.
Let me ask the mirror:
What will transpire?

Decisions always have an effect.
They create many pieces I must connect.
Every action opens up insight:
Perhaps, mistakes can be made right.
Can I find myself? I just might.

To be or not to be…
I need to live my life for me.
I will look for no one else to guide—
My instinct is where I will confide.
Because I am present a limited time,
I must try to live all of life at its prime.

When I look at the past, I feel ashamed.
I have no one in the world to blame
and no rock to crawl under and hide.
I thus come away standing with my pride.
Now, with life seen through *my* sight,
can I find myself? I just might.

Which bookshelf has the answer?
The answer is not in any volume.
It's deep within oneself.

Kick

The Curve Ball

Life can throw a curve ball:
We break a leg and down we fall,
our plans dissolved to nothing at all.

This tense and tangled mindset
makes our goals so easy to forget.
Detour: destination not to be seen yet.

But our unwavering spirits are hard to kill.
Even facing a rigorous climb up a hill
with our strides forced to a standstill.

When everything seems out of control—
just kick the rocks and begin to roll.
Back on the move…no time to stroll.

We diverge from our first path; we ignore distraction
and think ahead with an alternate plan of action.
Reaching the goal? The ultimate satisfaction.

Listen

Keep Your Ear to the Ground

Death will stop our breath one day.
Many will wish for an extended stay.
So, live every moment—laugh, love, and play.

When I was young, I wished to be older.
I grew up and became a bit bolder.
The world then was cold, but now it is colder.

Have patience…. Take it slow.
Living words are about to flow.
Here is what I have come to know:

No place is too safe, including here.
Have watchful eyes, no matter where.
Trust your intuition in any atmosphere.

But make decisions solely on fact.
One reckless act can have lasting impact.
So, think intensely before you choose to act.

Truth or dare, life is no game.
Diverse people, different in thought and name.
Seek out why into your life they came.

Walk forward, but don't be led by the blind.
You won't need to go back or glance behind.
Influences, good and bad, are easy to find.

Another word of advice:
Be nice, but not too nice.
Others' happiness is at what sacrifice?

I listened to the wise, I will admit.
Through their lessons of relentless grit,
I'm wiser now. Take my word for it.

Return

Haven

I have searched the earth far and deep
and found nowhere I can soundly sleep—
except in this simple but elegant space
with its table full of food to grace.
Whether I sit in a chair or lie on the floor,
no feeling compares once I open the door.

From the ceiling hang glass-blown fixtures,
on the wall, hand-painted pictures.
The energy of peace is a serenade
that causes every single shadow to fade
and shapes the smile upon my face.
Homesick, I return at a hasty pace.

I feel comfort; I have nothing to fear.
Inside, love draws me near.
External noise? That's sound my ears don't hear.
The place to be jovial, the place to shed a tear,
home always says "Welcome" to me.
There's no other place I would rather be.

Predict

The Queen of Nature

Listen as the wind blows.
It whispers words we don't know.
Feel the rain as it drops.
The rain dances nonstop.
The sun shines after thunder.
Nature is a secret wonder.
Snow falls into a flake
while water freezes in the lake.
The leaves turn brown and green.
Nature is crowned ruler: Queen.

Her scepter spins and makes the earth shake.
I wonder if the sleeping will awake.
The stars fall from a faraway mile.
The night moon perches for a short while.
Nature again writes her own story
when she awakes at morning's glory.
Queen Nature can be quiet and still
or take on the role of a combative shrill.
People try to predict her, to make a forecast.
She never speaks first; her word's always last.
Her shadow's in the lightning she will cast.
She is Nature. She is not steadfast.

Triumph

The Test

My heart thumps under distress.
Anxiety runs rabid against my zest.
The tears erupt, I unwillingly confess.
I, in triumph, trample the test.
I pass! Even after making that wild guess.
Disheveled in my stance, I need to rest.
Marvelous peace soothes my melancholy mess.
Though time constantly ticks inside my chest,
I can't do anything more—or anything less.
Bubbles burst outward from my internal best.
When much is required, the result is success.
This is given: I travel through life as its guest.

Receive

My Home Is Your Home

One Saturday morning, Tia arrived at the retirement home to start her weekend shift. After she clocked in, she walked down the hallway to make sure all of the residents in her wing were up and ready for breakfast. As she went from room to room and greeted everyone, they smiled and chatted with her briefly as she handed out their newspapers.

The last room Tia visited belonged to Mrs. B, who had been a resident at the home since her husband's death twelve years before. Mrs. B's children lived far away and didn't visit much, so she had become very fond of Tia over the eight years Tia had worked there, treating her as if she were her own granddaughter. As soon as Tia walked in that day, Mrs. B made a special request.

"Tia, I would like to go to my house today for a short visit. Will you have time to drive me?"

"Yes," Tia replied, "but we'll have to wait and go about four p.m. And because of my schedule, we can't stay more than an hour."

"Okay, that's fine. I will be ready right at four o'clock." Mrs. B. smiled. "It's time for me to go back. I haven't seen that house in about five years."

Tia's morning was busy as she served breakfast and passed out medications, but the rest of the day was quiet as she made sure all of her residents had what they needed. Mrs. B, though, was so excited about visiting her house, she talked about it all day. As she had promised, she was waiting for Tia at the door at four p.m. in her best hat, coat, gloves—and holding on tight to her favorite cane.

During the trip, Mrs. B told stories of raising her children and shared several of her holiday memories. When Tia finally pulled into the driveway of the regal, two-story house, Mrs. B stared at it for a minute through the windshield. "This is where I lived for thirty years. The rest of me is no longer here, bur my heart is still here. And sometimes you just have to go back to where your heart lives."

Mrs. B pulled her house key out of her coat pocket while Tia moved around the car to open the door and help her from the seat. Mrs. B stood and stared for another ten seconds at her house and then used her cane to walk down the sidewalk to the entrance. When Mrs. B's arthritis pain kept her from gripping the key, Tia helped her unlock the front door.

As soon as they entered the house, Mrs. B walked toward her piano and sat on the bench in front of it. She uncovered the keys and touched them as if she wanted to play, but instead just rested her hands. Slowly, she turned her body and let her eyes move around the room, observing every detail. Dusty, antique furnishings sat on the worn hardwood floors. Old cobwebbed curtains hung at the 50-year old windows and made it appear, from the outside, that someone was still living there. Tia was right by her side as they walked through the downstairs, headed up the staircase, and visited every room upstairs. The tour convinced Tia that Mrs. B had been a woman of elegant style and had spared no expense.

"I have wonderful memories of the life I lived here. I always hoped this house would serve as home to another family one day." Mrs. B sat on the corner of one of the beds for a few minutes and ran her hand back and forth over the coverlet. "Tia, I'm ready to go. I'm getting tired." She smiled and said, "Leave the light on for me."

"Okay, Mrs. B. Let's go back."

They slowly walked downstairs and through the front door. After Mrs. B locked the door, she turned to Tia. "I have something to tell you. I brought you here today for two reasons. First, I wanted to see my house for the last time. The other reason is that I know you have a young family. Tia, I am ninety-eight years old and this chapter of my life has closed. But you can start a new chapter in your life. Why not begin it here?"

"Where is 'here'?"

Mrs. B replied, "Here is in this house. You have taken care of me for many years, and now I want my home to be your home." She handed the house key to Tia.

Tia took the key and hugged Mrs. B. She felt sad that their visit to the house had caused Mrs. B to become so sentimental. Right now, though, she felt it best to pretend she would accept the gift. "Are you sure?" she asked with a smile.

Mrs. B said again, "My home is your home."

On the way back to the retirement home, they were both rather quiet. About halfway there, Mrs. B reached over and touched

Tia's arm. "Your family will be so happy there." After she escorted Mrs. B back to her room, Tia gave her an extra long hug.

"Have a good night, Mrs. B. Thank you for the wonderful gift." She then went home to discuss the day's strange events with her family.

The next day Tia began her morning routine and greeted all her residents. When she reached Mrs. B's room, the door was open. She knocked as usual and called out. "Mrs. B…," but Mrs. B did not answer. Tia entered the room to find an empty bed.

Surprised, and instantly upset, Tia used her cell phone to call Janet, her supervisor. When Janet heard Tia's voice, she asked Tia to come to the office. As soon as she looked at Janet's face, Tia knew the worst had happened. Janet reached for her hand and said, "She passed quickly—sometime during night. We are all going to miss her." Tia burst into tears.

"Mrs. B will always live in our hearts." said Janet. "Mrs. B loved you, you know."

"I do know," said Tia. "She even tried to give me her house key last night. Here it is."

Janet smiled and said, "Tia, you can keep that key."

"What do you mean I can keep the key?"

"Mrs. B really did mean for you to have her house. She told us a while back about her plans and made sure all the legal paperwork was completed before she took you there yesterday."

It took a while for Tia to recover in Janet's office, but she finally made her way back to the hallway. Although a feeling of peace came upon Tia as she returned to Mrs. B's room, her sense of loss was overpowering.

"Why did she have to go so soon? I didn't even get to fix her raisin bran this morning." she whispered. A moment later she burst again into tears.

When she could finally compose herself, Tia looked around at all the beautiful items in the room and found that she had sat down on one of Mrs. B's favorite pieces of furniture: her makeup chair. Remembering the times she had helped Mrs. B put on makeup in that chair helped Tia manage a smile for the mirror in front of her. As soon as she smiled, she seemed to hear a familiar voice in her ear.

"My home is your home!"

Inspire

The Dream

One misty night, I fell deep
Into a dream sleep.

A paper scroll was placed at my side.
I read its words: Whom can you guide?

When that question was presented to me,
I knew whom, what, and how I should be.

Without delay, I rose to my feet.
I knew a lost word and I were to meet.

For twenty days, I did not thirst, did not eat
as my soul created thoughts with each pulsating beat.

That mesmerizing memory, day and night I now keep.
And I hold that scroll close—especially as I sleep.

Kalliope

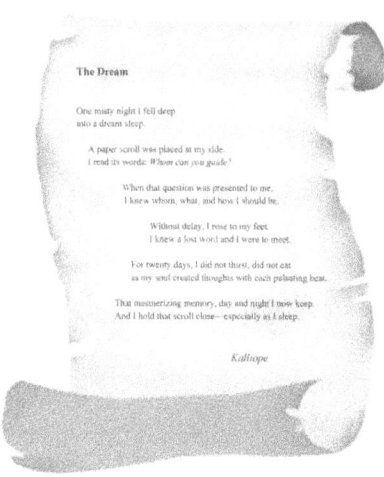

Title Index

A Lazy Day *41*
A Nurse's Creed *39*
A Working Man He Was: FATHER *15*

Believe *31*
Best Friends Forever *25*

Can You Remember? MOTHER *7*

Dear Husband-to-Be *21*

Fall 2014 *57*
Father *19*

Happy Birth-Day *29*
Haven *65*
Hurt *33*

I Will *43*

Joy *45*

Keep Your Ear to the Ground *63*

Me *37*
Mother *13*
My Home Is Your Home *71*

Rise *27*

Seasons Change *23*
Show Me Myself *59*
Strive *35*

Title Index continued

The Chef *53*
The Curse *49*
The Curve Ball *61*
The Dream *77*
The Journey to Elegance *1*
The Queen of Nature *67*
The Test *69*
Time *47*

Wisdom *55*
Words *51*

Yesterday *5*

www.ingramcontent.com/pod-product-compliance
Lightning Source LLC
Chambersburg PA
CBHW020018050426
42450CB00005B/535